Marthaler, Jon.
796.334   Ultimate soccer road trip
Mar

Book Level 5.7
Quiz 501308

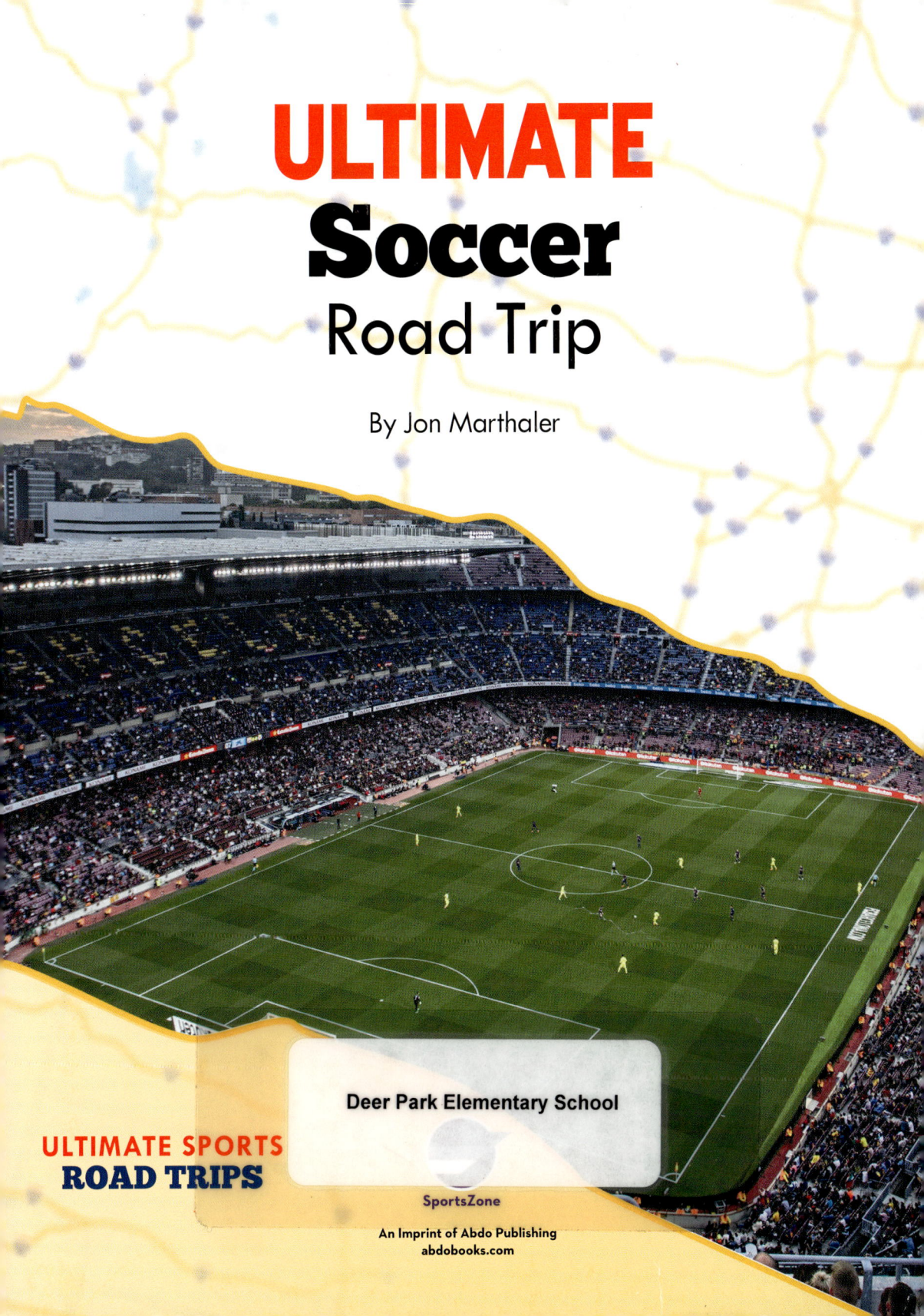

ULTIMATE Soccer Road Trip

By Jon Marthaler

ULTIMATE SPORTS ROAD TRIPS

SportsZone
An Imprint of Abdo Publishing
abdobooks.com

ABDOBOOKS.COM

Published by Abdo Publishing, a division of ABDO, PO Box 398166, Minneapolis, Minnesota 55439. Copyright © 2019 by Abdo Consulting Group, Inc. International copyrights reserved in all countries. No part of this book may be reproduced in any form without written permission from the publisher. SportsZone™ is a trademark and logo of Abdo Publishing.

Printed in the United States of America, North Mankato, Minnesota
092018
012019

THIS BOOK CONTAINS RECYCLED MATERIALS

Cover Photo: Xavier Bonilla/NurPhoto/Sipa USA
Interior Photos: Xavier Bonilla/NurPhoto/Sipa USA, 1; KYDPL Kyodo/AP Images, 4–5; Invicta Kent Media/Rex Features, 7; Popperfoto/Getty Images, 8, 45; Gary M. Prior/Allsport/Getty Images Sport/Getty Images, 11; Thomas Boyd/The Oregonian/AP Images, 13; Craig Mitchelldyer/ISI/Rex Features, 14; Ulrike Stein/Shutterstock Images, 17; Jamie McDonald/FIFA/Getty Images, 18; Staff/AFP/Getty Images, 20–21; Rafael Martin-Gaitero/Shutterstock Images, 23, 44; Goran Bogicevic/Shutterstock Images, 24–25; STF/AFP/Getty Images, 27; Ian Walton/Getty Images Sport/Getty Images, 28; Caro/Andreas Muhs/Newscom, 31; Peter Kneffel/picture-alliance/dpa/AP Images, 32; Blom UK/Getty Images, 35; Christian Bertrand/Shutterstock Images, 36; Shutterstock Images, 39; Rafael Ramirez Lee/Shutterstock Images, 40–41; John Walton/Press Association URN:26055584/AP Images, 43

Editor: Bradley Cole
Series Designer: Melissa Martin

Library of Congress Control Number: 2018949189

Publisher's Cataloging-in-Publication Data

Names: Marthaler, Jon, author.
Title: Ultimate soccer road trip / by Jon Marthaler.
Description: Minneapolis, Minnesota : Abdo Publishing, 2019 | Series: Ultimate sports road trips | Includes online resources and index.
Identifiers: ISBN 9781532117572 (lib. bdg.) | ISBN 9781532170430 (ebook)
Subjects: LCSH: Sports arenas--Juvenile literature. | Sports spectators--Juvenile literature. | Soccer--Juvenile literature.
Classification: DDC 796.334068--dc23

TABLE OF CONTENTS

INTRODUCTION
GOOOOAAAAAAL!........................... 4

CHAPTER 1
OLD TRAFFORD................................ 6

CHAPTER 2
PROVIDENCE PARK......................... 12

CHAPTER 3
ESTADIO AZTECA............................ 16

CHAPTER 4
ESTADIO ALBERTO J. ARMANDO...... 22

CHAPTER 5
FNB STADIUM 26

CHAPTER 6
ALLIANZ ARENA............................. 30

CHAPTER 7
CAMP NOU..................................... 34

CHAPTER 8
ESTADIO SANTIAGO BERNABÉU....... 38

MAP 44   ONLINE RESOURCES . . . 47

GLOSSARY. 46   INDEX 48

MORE INFORMATION. . . 47   ABOUT THE AUTHOR . . 48

INTRO

Gooooaaaaaaal!

Soccer is the world's most popular sport. And almost every country on Earth has at least one amazing soccer venue. No other sport can boast so many huge, famous stadiums across the globe.

The best stadiums are home to some of the world's best soccer teams. The greatest players in history have made their names on these fields. Some of the most famous games ever played took place there too. World Cups have been played in these stadiums. Some stadiums have hosted the final of the Champions League. Some are known for their incredibly loud fans. Others are famous for what has happened on the pitch.

The cathedrals of soccer include the largest stadiums on two continents. The road trip will visit a stadium called "the Theatre of Dreams" in England, a stadium nicknamed after a box of chocolates, and another that started life as a track stadium. What they all have in common is soccer, the "Beautiful Game."

Argentina fans celebrate during the 2018 World Cup.

OLD TRAFFORD

Soccer was invented in England. England's soccer leagues and tournaments have been active for more than 100 years. Naturally, England also has some of the oldest stadiums in the world. Many of the richest, oldest teams in the world come from England. Old Trafford's history starts all the way back in 1908, a year before the stadium was built.

Manchester United has long been the richest team in England. Other people called the team "Moneybags United" because the team could spend so much to acquire talented players. Many people were moving into Manchester for work in factories. The population had grown to more than 2 million people. So the club built a new stadium

FUN FACT

Old Trafford was bombed by Germany during World War II (1939–1945). The main stand was destroyed and the pitch was wrecked. Manchester United had to play its home games at rival Manchester City's stadium for eight years before Old Trafford could be rebuilt.

OLD TRAFFORD

Manchester, England

Date Opened: 1909
Capacity: 74,994
Home Team: Manchester United

Bobby Charlton, *left*, Denis Law (10), and George Best (33) were three of the best players to ever call Old Trafford home.

with room for 80,000 fans. United's owner told the architect to make it "the finest stadium in the North." It was finished in 1909. More than 100 years later, Old Trafford still has the largest capacity of any Premier League stadium.

Manchester United has won more league titles than any other team in England. Some of the best players in English soccer history have called Old Trafford home: George Best, Denis Law, Bobby Charlton, Ryan Giggs, and David Beckham. Best, Charlton, and Law are known as the "Holy Trinity" of Manchester United. They were three of the best soccer players to ever wear the Manchester United jersey. A statue of the three of them together stands outside the stadium. Former managers Alex Ferguson and Matt Busby are also honored with statues nearby.

Most of England's biggest matches are played in Wembley Stadium. But Old Trafford is also regularly used for important events. It hosted the semifinals of the 1996 European Championships and the semifinals of the 2012 Olympic soccer competitions. England's national team played many of its matches there when Wembley was being rebuilt between 2002 and 2007. The most famous England team match at Old Trafford came in 2001. England needed a win or draw against Greece to qualify for the World Cup. With the clock

FUN FACT

Bobby Charlton is credited with nicknaming the stadium "the Theatre of Dreams" because of how good Manchester United was and how many big games they won. He once admitted that it was probably a journalist who came up with the nickname, not him.

ticking, England was losing 2–1. David Beckham, who starred for Manchester United, stepped up to take a free kick 30 yards from the goal. He launched a bending kick that flew over the wall of defenders and into the top corner! The game ended in a draw, sending England through to the World Cup.

In more than 100 years, Manchester United has won 19 Premier League and First Division titles, 11 Football Association (FA) Cup titles, and three European Cups while playing at Old Trafford. With success like that, United won't be moving anywhere else for a while. A century from now, Old Trafford will still likely be one of the largest, most famous stadiums in the world.

David Beckham's free kick against Greece helped send England's national team to the World Cup.

2 PROVIDENCE PARK

As of 2018, the Portland Timbers have only been a Major League Soccer (MLS) team for seven years. The Portland Thorns have played at Providence Park for only five years. But the history of the stadium goes all the way back to 1926.

Providence Park was originally called Multnomah Stadium. It was built by an athletic club in Portland. All kinds of events have been in the stadium, including football and dog racing. For many years it was a minor league baseball stadium. The Portland Timbers first played soccer there in 1975. When the Timbers joined MLS, the stadium was rebuilt. Now it mainly houses soccer matches.

Portland has sold out every MLS game it has ever played at Providence Park. The Thorns draw bigger crowds than any other National Women's Soccer League (NWSL) team. The fans sing songs and chant for the entire game. The stadium has a wooden roof, and the sound of chanting and singing bounces off the roof.

PROVIDENCE PARK

Portland, Oregon, USA

Date Opened: 1926
Capacity: 21,144
Home Teams: Portland Timbers and Portland Thorns

It makes Providence Park the loudest stadium in both MLS and NWSL. Those fans are the reason that Portland has earned the nickname "Soccer City USA."

 Fans at Providence Park help give the stadium its festive atmosphere.

Beyond the play on the pitch, Providence Park provides fans with plenty of reasons to come to games. The food at the stadium is top notch. Fans can get street tacos, BBQ sandwiches, gourmet mac and cheese, and even a vegan option for burgers. There are also food carts that bring the food around the stadium, so it's easy for fans to grab a bite and never miss a minute of the game.

> **FUN FACT**
>
> Before they played in MLS, the Portland Timbers played in the North American Soccer League. In 1977, Providence Park—then called Civic Stadium—hosted the Soccer Bowl, the league's championship game. Pelé, the greatest soccer player ever, helped the New York Cosmos win the title. It was his last professional match.

On April 14, 2011, the Timbers played their first-ever home game in MLS. Fans lifted a huge banner before the game that called the Timbers the "King of Clubs." Portland beat Chicago 4–2 that night.

Providence Park is not the biggest soccer stadium in the United States. But it is still the best soccer stadium in the United States, because of its history and its loud, excited fans.

ESTADIO AZTECA

Estadio Azteca is the only stadium in the world that has hosted two World Cup finals. The championship matches in 1970 and 1986 were played there. Azteca also is the home of Club América, the most famous team in Mexico. And all of the home games for the Mexican national team are played there as well.

> **FUN FACT**
> Tours are available seven days a week (except on game days) at Estadio Azteca that include visits to the press room, dressing room, and dugout.

Azteca was built in 1966. Club América was getting bigger and more popular. Mexico planned to be the home of the 1968 Olympics. So Club América's owner decided to build a huge stadium for his team and for Mexico's national team. When it was finished, it held almost 115,000 fans. It has since been remodeled to add more luxury areas for fans and media areas for Fédération Internationale de Football Association (FIFA) and National Football

ESTADIO AZTECA

Mexico City, Mexico

Date Opened: 1966
Capacity: 87,000
Home Teams: Club América, Cruz Azul, and the Mexico national team

 Crowds wait with anticipation in Azteca for the final 2011 Under-17 World Cup match between Uruguay and Mexico.

League (NFL) games. The new spaces came at the expense of regular seating and decreased the capacity to 87,000 people.

It is hard for visiting teams to play at Azteca. Mexico City is more than a mile (1.6 km) above sea level. The air contains less oxygen at that altitude. Players tire out faster if they're not used to working hard in that atmosphere. Also, Mexico City has poor air quality in general due to pollution.

The final match of the 1970 World Cup was one of the most famous matches in World Cup history. It matched Brazil and Italy. Brazil was the best offensive team in the world, and had Pelé, the best soccer player ever. Italy was known for being great at defense. It was good offense versus good defense. Brazil won, 4–1, and Pelé scored one goal and set up another.

In 1986, Argentina beat West Germany 3–2 in the final at Azteca. The quarterfinal match between England and Argentina, also held at the stadium, might be even more famous. Argentina's Diego Maradona scored both goals in a 2–1 win. The first is known as the "Hand of God" goal. Maradona jumped in front of England goalkeeper Peter Shilton and unintentionally deflected the ball over him and into the net with his hand. After the game, Maradona said the goal was scored "a little with the head of Maradona, and a little with the hand of God." The second goal was named the "Goal of the Century" in 2002. Maradona got the ball in his own half of the field. He dribbled past four England players. He then faked his way past Shilton and scored.

> **FUN FACT**
> The Mexico national team has been playing at Azteca since 1966. In all of that time, it has lost only twice at home in World Cup qualifying matches. Its first home loss wasn't until 2001.

 Classic soccer moments such as Maradona's Goal of the Century have happened in Estadio Azteca.

Club América has been successful playing at Estadio Azteca. As of 2018, 11 of its 12 Mexican league titles have come since the team moved to Azteca in 1966. The club also has thrived in Confederation of North, Central American and Caribbean Association Football (CONCACAF) regional play, winning the

CONCACAF Champions Cup/CONCACAF Champions League seven times. With the great home-field advantage that Azteca provides, América, Cruz Azul, and the Mexico national team will always be hard to beat.

ESTADIO ALBERTO J. ARMANDO

Boca Juniors does not have the largest stadium in South America. The team doesn't even have the largest stadium in Argentina. But "La Bombonera," as everyone calls it, might be the loudest stadium in the whole world. The fans are so loud that the ground shakes.

La Bombonera was built in a residential neighborhood in Buenos Aires. Because there wasn't much space available, the stadium was built up, not out. It makes it look like the field is surrounded by walls of people. Three sides of the stadium look like a regular stadium. But the fourth is a vertical wall of seats and luxury boxes. The fans are almost right on top of the field.

> **FUN FACT**
>
> La Bombonera means "the chocolate box." The stadium got its nickname when the architect realized that it looked like the chocolate he was eating—flat on one side and rounded on the other three sides.

ESTADIO ALBERTO J. ARMANDO

Buenos Aires, Argentina

Date Opened: 1940
Capacity: 49,000
Home Team: Boca Juniors

 **La Bombonera's steep seating keeps fans close to the action.**

Boca Juniors has a huge rivalry with River Plate, its crosstown rival. People call this match "El Superclásico," the Super Classic. The Super Classic matches rotate between La Bombonera and River Plates' El Monumental. Argentina's best player ever, Diego Maradona, played for Boca in this match in 1981 and again between 1995 and 1997. There is a statue of him in the team's museum at the stadium.

Boca Juniors faced rival River Plate for the 2001 Copa Libertadores final. Boca had won the first game of the series in Mexico City, but River Plate won Game 2 at La Bombonera.

The teams were tied after two games, but Boca Juniors finished off their rival in the penalty shootout, winning 3–1.

La Bombonera is regularly listed among the 10 best soccer stadiums in the world for spectators. In 2015, English magazine *FourFourTwo* named it the No. 1 stadium in the world. Don't ask visiting players, though. They voted it the "most feared" stadium to play in. Boca Juniors' passionate fans are that intense. Even though La Bombonera is not the biggest stadium, it will probably always be the loudest.

FNB STADIUM

FNB Stadium is the largest stadium in Africa. It hosts not only the South African national team and the Kaizer Chiefs FC, but also some of the most important events in South Africa. Nelson Mandela's first speech after he was released from prison in 1990 was at FNB Stadium. The stadium also hosted Mandela's memorial service in 2013.

The most important matches played at FNB are those between Kaizer Chiefs FC and the Orlando Pirates. Kaizer Motaung was once a star for the Pirates. He went to play in the United States for a team named the Atlanta Chiefs. In 1969, there was a dispute at Orlando. Three players and a coach were kicked out. Motaung went home to try to fix things. But he could not succeed. So he started a new team called the Kaizer XI. It played some friendly games and was very popular. So Motaung decided to permanently start a new team: Kaizer Chiefs FC. It became one of the best teams in South Africa.

FNB STADIUM

Johannesburg, South Africa

Date Opened: 1989
Capacity: 94,736
Home Teams: Kaizer Chiefs and the South Africa national team

The stadium was rebuilt in 2009 for the 2010 World Cup. It housed eight matches, including the championship. The final was between Spain and the Netherlands. It set a record with 14 yellow

Efe Ambrose of Nigeria chases the ball in the 2013 Africa Cup of Nations final at FNB Stadium.

cards, including two for Dutch defender John Heitinga, who was sent off. The match went to extra time. With just four minutes to go, Spain's Andrés Iniesta scored and Spain held on for a 1–0 victory.

> **FUN FACT**
> The stadium is nicknamed "The Calabash," a word for an African pot. It has panels on the outside of the stadium that make it look like a large pot. At night when the stadium is lit up, it looks like a star-lit sky.

In many ways, FNB Stadium is the most important stadium in Africa. The World Cup has been played on the continent only once. It seems fitting that the continent's biggest stadium played host for its biggest game.

ALLIANZ ARENA

Bayern Munich is one of the biggest teams in the world. For many years, it played its home games at the Olympic Stadium in Munich, Germany. Before the World Cup came to Germany in 2006, the club decided it was time to build something newer and better. It partnered with its crosstown rival 1860 Munich, which also played at the Olympic Stadium. The two clubs jointly built the Allianz Arena.

The new stadium opened in 2005. The next year, six World Cup matches were played there. One of these matches was France's semifinal win against Portugal.

FUN FACT

Bayern Munich no longer shares the stadium with 1860. In 2008, Bayern bought out the smaller club and now owns the stadium by itself. In 2017, 1860 moved to a different stadium.

ALLIANZ ARENA

Munich, Germany

Date Opened: 2005
Capacity: 75,000
Home Team: Bayern Munich

 FC Bayern Munich beat FC Porto at home in the Champions League quarterfinal in 2015.

Since moving to the Allianz Arena, Bayern has been fantastic. The club amazingly has won nine of the 13 Bundesliga championships and seven of their 13 German Cups.

Bayern almost won the Champions League final at home in 2012. It played the finals against Chelsea, which took home the title in a shootout. Bayern's Bastian Schweinsteiger missed his penalty kick, and Chelsea went 5-for-5 on its penalties to win it.

Great players such as Schweinsteiger, Thomas Müller, Robert Lewandowski, Arjen Robben, Franck Ribéry, and Manuel Neuer have played for Bayern at Allianz Arena. Those players' greatest moment at the Allianz came in the 2015 Champions League quarterfinals against FC Porto of Portugal. Bayern came into the game trailing 3–1 after the first match of the series. It needed to win by at least two goals to move on to the next round. Bayern blitzed Porto, scoring four times in the first half. They ran away to a 6–1 win as the crowd roared.

> **FUN FACT**
> The outside of the stadium is covered in panels that can change color. When Bayern plays there, the stadium is lit up red. The local government had to stop the stadium from changing color during the day because it was causing multiple car accidents from distracted drivers.

As of 2018, Bayern has won six consecutive Bundesliga titles. Its 2018 title came after it won the league by an incredible 21 points. Bayern looks like it will dominate Germany at the Allianz Arena for years to come.

CAMP NOU

The largest stadium in Europe belongs to FC Barcelona, one of the most famous teams in the entire world. The club won the Spanish league championship in 1947–48 and in 1948–49. The team got so popular that it decided to build a large stadium. When the stadium was finished, more than 93,000 fans could cheer on FC Barcelona.

The biggest games at the Camp Nou are those between Barcelona and Real Madrid, the two best teams in the Spanish league. Barcelona is also the best team from Catalonia, which is a part of Spain that wants to break away and form its own country. Madrid is Spain's capital city, and Real is the most popular club for people who want to keep Spain together. So the rivalry resonates equally on and off

> **FUN FACT**
>
> Camp Nou means "New Ground" in Catalan, the official language of Barcelona. This means that fans have been calling the stadium "new ground" for more than 60 years.

CAMP NOU

Barcelona, Spain

Date Opened: 1957
Capacity: 99,354
Home Team: FC Barcelona

the field. People call these games "El Clásico," the Classic. The Barcelona fans are never louder than when their team is beating Real Madrid.

 **FC Barcelona games at the Camp Nou always draw a crowd.**

The best player in Camp Nou history is Lionel Messi. As of 2018, he had scored more than 500 goals for Barcelona. He has also scored more goals in El Clásico matches than any other player in history. He will be a hero at the Camp Nou for many years to come, even after he stops playing.

Barcelona's slogan is "More than a club." The yellow seats at the Camp Nou spell it out in the Catalan language: "Més que un club." The passionate fans that pack the Camp Nou make it more than just an ordinary stadium, too.

> **FUN FACT**
> The club plans to add even more seats to the Camp Nou in 2021 so that 105,000 fans can attend. A new roof will catch the rain so that the water can be used on the field.

ESTADIO SANTIAGO BERNABÉU

The Estadio Santiago Bernabéu, usually called just "the Bernabéu," is one of the biggest stadiums in Spain. It has hosted a World Cup final and a European Championships final. Spain's national team regularly plays there too. In 2010 it was the site of the fourth Union of European Football Associations (UEFA) Champions League final. But the Bernabéu is mostly famous because of Real Madrid. No other club has won more Spanish league titles. No other club has won the UEFA Champions League more often.

The man the stadium is named after did almost everything for the club. Santiago Bernabéu played for Real Madrid until 1927. He later was the manager of the team. He became president of Real Madrid in 1943. At the time, Real Madrid had won La Liga (the Spanish league) only twice. Barcelona and Atlético Madrid were better and more famous. Bernabéu remodeled the team. He hired

ESTADIO SANTIAGO BERNABÉU

Madrid, Spain

Date Opened: 1947
Capacity: 81,044
Home Team: Real Madrid CF

 **Fans consistently pack the Bernabéu to watch Real Madrid play.**

scouts to find better players and bring them to Real. Some of the best players in the world came to Real Madrid, including Alfredo di Stefano of Argentina and Hungarian striker Ferenc Puskás.

Bernabéu thought that the team needed a new stadium to match its new approach. He convinced the club to build a new

stadium on the site of its old one. The new one was much bigger and much nicer. It opened in 1947, but Bernabéu got the club to keep building. By the time he was done, in 1954, the stadium could hold 125,000 people. In 1955, the club's members voted to name the stadium after the president who helped build it.

Italy and West Germany played for the 1982 World Cup in Bernabéu. The West German squad played well in the first half, but neither team scored. Then Italy took over. Italy scored off a header at 57 minutes. Then, in the 69th minute, Italy pushed its advantage to 2–0. West Germany tried to push back but the Italian defense was too much. After clearing a West German attack, Italy countered aggressively down the right side of the pitch and scored again in the 81st minute. West Germany would go on to score two minutes later off a rebound, but Italy's lead was too big.

One of the most memorable players to ever call the Bernabéu home was forward Cristiano Ronaldo. His best night at the Bernabéu came in 2016. Real Madrid was playing VfL Wolfsburg, from Germany, in the quarterfinals of the Champions League. Madrid was expected to win easily. But Real lost the first leg of the match 2–0 at Wolfsburg.

In the second leg, though, Ronaldo led his team back. He scored twice in the first 20 minutes to tie the total score. Then, with just

> **FUN FACT**
> Bernabéu helped convince European soccer teams to set up the European Cup competition between the champions of each country's league. The tournament began in 1955. Real Madrid won the cup in each of the first five years.

Cristiano Ronaldo puts one past the keeper for Real Madrid in front of his home crowd.

14 minutes left in the game, he lined up for a free kick. The fans held their breath. Ronaldo ran up and chipped the ball past the wall of defenders. It bounced past the goalkeeper and into the net. His hat trick gave his team a 3–2 win. Real Madrid went on to win the Champions League that season. Even as Real Madrid's famous players come and go, the Bernabéu will always be a special stadium for soccer fans.

MAP

1. **Old Trafford.** Manchester, England
2. **Providence Park.** Portland, Oregon, USA
3. **Estadio Azteca.** Mexico City, Mexico
4. **Estadio Alberto J. Armando.** Buenos Aires, Argentina

5. **FNB Stadium.** Johannesburg, South Africa
6. **Allianz Arena.** Munich, Germany
7. **Camp Nou.** Barcelona, Spain
8. **Estadio Santiago Bernabéu.** Madrid, Spain

Glossary

Champions League
An interleague competition for the best teams in Europe.

dribble
To touch the ball with the feet as it is taken up the field.

extra time
Two 15-minute periods added to a game if the score is tied at the end of regulation.

free kick
An unguarded kick awarded to a team after a foul.

hat trick
Three goals by the same player in one game.

penalty kick
A play in which a shooter faces a goalkeeper alone; it is used to decide tie games or as a result of a foul.

pitch
The soccer field.

sent off
Thrown out of the game, either for two cautions (yellow cards) or one ejection (red card).

World Cup
The biggest soccer tournament in the world, held once every four years among national teams.

yellow card
A caution given to a player by a referee for playing dangerously or behaving badly.

More Information

BOOKS

Kortemeier, Todd. *Real Madrid CF*. Minneapolis, MN: Abdo Publishing, 2018.

Marthaler, Jon. *FC Bayern Munich*. Minneapolis, MN: Abdo Publishing, 2018.

Trusdell, Brian. *Pelé: Soccer Star & Ambassador*. Minneapolis, MN: Abdo Publishing, 2014.

Online Resources

To learn more about soccer stadiums, visit **abdobooklinks.com**. These links are routinely monitored and updated to provide the most current information available.

Index

Allianz Arena, 30–33

Bayern Munich, 30–33
Beckham, David, 9–10
Bernabéu, Santiago, 38–41, 42
Best, George, 9
Boca Juniors, 22–25

Camp Nou, 34–37
Charlton, Bobby, 9
Club América, 16, 20
Cruz Azul, 16, 20

Estadio Alberto J. Armando, 22–25
Estadio Azteca, 16–21
Estadio Santiago Bernabéu, 38–43

FC Barcelona, 34–37
FNB Stadium, 26–29

Kaizer Chiefs FC, 26

Law, Denis, 9

Manchester United, 6–10
Mandela, Nelson, 26
Maradona, Diego, 19, 24
Messi, Lionel, 37
Mexico national team, 19, 21
Motaung, Kaizer, 26

Old Trafford, 6–10

Pelé, 15, 19
Portland Thorns, 12
Portland Timbers, 12, 15
Providence Park, 12–15

Real Madrid CF, 34, 36, 38–43
Ronaldo, Cristiano, 42–43

Shilton, Peter, 19

About the Author

Jon Marthaler has been a freelance sportswriter for more than 15 years. He writes a weekly soccer column for the *Star Tribune* in Minneapolis, Minnesota. Jon lives in St. Paul, Minnesota, with his wife and their daughter.